WHAT SONS TEACH US

WHAT SONS TEACH US

Life's Lessons Learned From Our Boys

 Willow Creek Press

Published by Willow Creek Press
P.O. Box 147, Minocqua, Wisconsin 54548

Editor: Andrea Donner

Photo Credits

© **Peter Arnold, Inc.:** p.6 © Nomi Baumgartl/Bilderberg; p.10 © Bart Harris/The Medical File;
p.13 © Rene Spalek/Bilderberg; p.14 © Andrej Reiser/Bilderberg; p.18 © Angelika Jakob/Bilderberg;
p.22 © Rene Spalek/Bilderberg; p.26 © Peter Mathis/Bilderberg; p.30 © Lynda Richardson;
p.33 © Peter Hirth/Transit; p.37 © Jean-Michel Labat/Phone; p.38 © Mike Schröder/Argus;
p.41 © Jeff Greenberg; p.42 © Carl R. Sams II; p.66 © John Cancalosi; p.69 © Jeff Greenberg;
p.73 © Christoph Busse/Transit

© **Norvia Behling:** pages 34, 85

© **Dusty Rose Kenny/www.thedustyimage.com:** page 54

© **Barbara Peacock/www.barbarapeacock.com:** pages 25, 29, 45, 50, 57, 62, 70, 74, 77, 81, 82, 86, 89, 90

Superstock: p.2 © age fotostock/SuperStock; p.17 © age fotostock/SuperStock;
p.21 © age fotostock/SuperStock; p.65 © age fotostock/SuperStock;
p.93 © maXx images/SuperStock; p.94 © age fotostock/SuperStock

Printed in Canada

While we try to teach our children all about life,
Our children teach us what life is all about.

Angela Schwindt

You can't plan the kind of deep love that results from having children.

Author unknown

affection

*We find delight in the beauty and happiness of children
that makes the heart too big for the body.*

Ralph Waldo Emerson

*What greater thing is there for human souls than
to feel that they are joined for life—
to be with each other in silent unspeakable memories.*

George Eliot

a m a z e m e n t

Every baby born into the world is a finer one than the last.

Charles Dickens

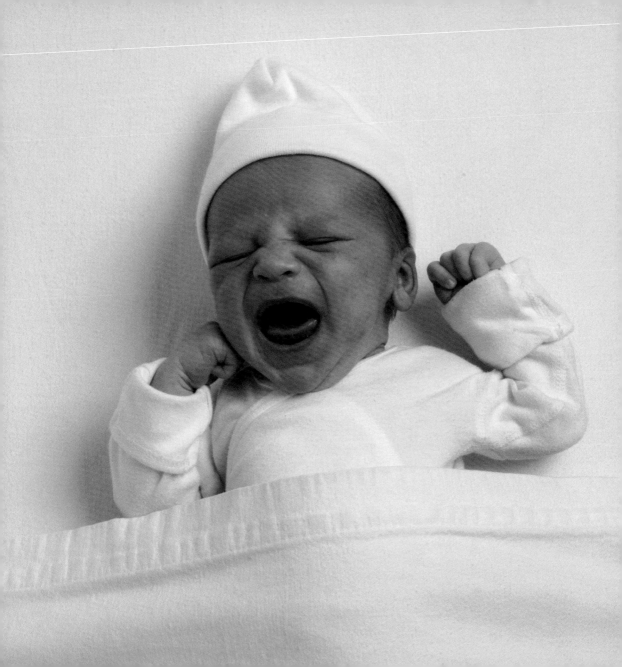

It sometimes happens, even in the best of families, that a baby is born.
This is not necessarily cause for alarm. The important thing
is to keep your wits about you and borrow some money.

Elinor Goulding Smith

bewilderment

Spread the diaper in the position of the diamond with you at bat. Then fold
second base down to home and set the baby on the pitcher's mound. Put first base
and third together, bring up home plate and pin the three together. Of course,
in case of rain, you gotta call the game and start all over again.

Jimmy Piersal, on how to diaper a baby, 1968

The only thing worth stealing is a kiss from a sleeping child.

Joe Houldsworth

b l e s s e d n e s s

Children are the bridge to heaven.

Persian proverb

In America there are two classes of travel—first class, and with children.

Robert Benchley

challenges

*Even when freshly washed and relieved of all obvious confections,
children tend to be sticky.*

Fran Lebowitz

It took me four years to paint like Raphael, but a lifetime to paint like a child.

Pablo Picasso

creativity

Creativity is a characteristic given to all human beings at birth.

Abraham Maslow

There is frequently more to be learned from the unexpected questions
of a child than the discourses of men.

John Locke

curiosity

Childhood is measured out by sounds and smells and sights,
before the dark hour of reason grows.

John Betjeman

With boys, you always know where you stand. Right in the path of a hurricane. It's all there. The fruit flies hovering over the waste can, the hamster trying to escape to cleaner air, the bedrooms decorated in Early Bus Station Restroom.

Erma Bombeck

daring

Of all the animals, the boy is the most unmanageable.

Plato

If you have never been hated by your child you have never been a parent.

Bette Davis

defiance

Any kid will run any errand for you if you ask at bedtime.

Red Skelton

You don't really understand human nature unless you know why a child on a merry-go-round will wave at his parents every time around— and why his parents will always wave back.

William D. Tammeus

enchantment

Children make you want to start life over.

Muhammad Ali

The hardest part of raising a child is teaching them to ride bicycles. A shaky child on a bicycle for the first time needs both support and freedom. The realization that this is what the child will always need can hit hard.

Sloan Wilson

encouragement

Whenever I held my newborn baby in my arms, I used to think that what I said and did to him could have an influence not only on him but on all whom he met, not only for a day or a month or a year, but for all eternity— a very challenging and exciting thought for a mother.

Rose Kennedy

Youth is a perpetual intoxication; it is a fever of the mind.

Francois Duc de la Rochefoucauld

e n e r g y

Boys are found everywhere—on top of, underneath, inside of, climbing on,
swinging from, running around or jumping to.

Alan Marshall Beck

The young and the old are closest to life.
They love every minute dearly.

Chief Dan George

e n j o y m e n t

That one is richest whose pleasures are cheapest.

Henry David Thoreau

There are children playing in the street who could solve some of my top problems in physics, because they have modes of sensory perception that I lost long ago.

J. Robert Oppenheimer

fearlessness

A boy is Truth with dirt on its face, Beauty with a cut on its finger, Wisdom with bubble gum in its hair, and the Hope of the future with a frog in its pocket.

Alan Marshall Beck

Kids: they dance before they learn there is anything that isn't music.

William Stafford

f u n

Only where children gather is there any real chance of fun.

Mignon McLaughlin

What feeling is so nice as a child's hand in yours? So small, so soft and warm,
like a kitten huddling in the shelter of your clasp.

Marjorie Holmes

gentleness

A child's hand in yours—what tenderness it arouses, what power it conjures.
You are instantly the very touchstone of wisdom and strength.

Marjorie Holmes

Childhood is the most beautiful of all life's seasons.

Author unknown

goodness

Raising boys has made me a more generous woman than I really am.
Undoubtedly, there are other routes to learning the wishes and dreams
of the presumably opposite sex, but I know of none more direct,
or more highly motivating, than being the mother of sons.

Mary Kay Blakely

Think what a better world it would be if we all, the whole world,
had cookies and milk about three o'clock every afternoon
and then lay down on our blankets for a nap.

Barbara Jordan

h a p p i n e s s

The only time I was truly happy was as a child,
before I knew what happiness was—or wasn't.

D.H. Mondfleur

When you teach your son, you teach your son's son.

The Talmud

heritage

Children are the living messages we send to a time we will not see.

John W. Whitehead

Children are a wonderful gift… They have an extraordinary capacity to see into the heart of things and to expose sham and humbug for what they are.

Desmond Tutu

honesty

Pretty much all the honest truth-telling there is in the world is done by children.

Oliver Wendell Holmes

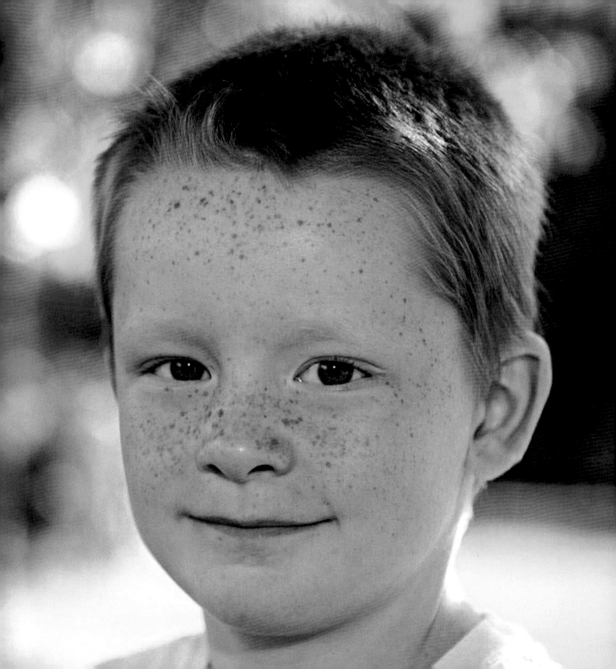

sweet childish days, that were as long
As twenty days are now.

William Wordsworth

i d l e n e s s

To fill the hour, that is happiness.

Ralph Waldo Emerson

There is a garden in every childhood, an enchanted place
where colors are brighter, the air softer,
and the morning more fragrant than ever again.

Elizabeth Lawrence

imagination

There are no seven wonders of the world in the eyes of a child.
There are seven million.

Walt Streightiff

A child's world is fresh and new and beautiful,
full of wonder and excitement.

Rachel Carson

innocence

Maybe that is why young people make success.
They don't know enough.

Richard P. Feynman

The older I get, the more I marvel at the wisdom of children.

David Morgan

intelligence

Our greatest natural resource is the minds of our children.

Walt Disney

A fairly bright boy is far more intelligent and far better
company than the average adult.

John B. S. Haldane

inventiveness

Children are like wet cement.
Whatever falls on them makes an impression.

Dr. Haim Ginott

Children have neither past nor future;
they enjoy the present, which very few of us do.

Jean de la Bruyere

joy

The older I grow the more earnestly I feel that the few joys
of childhood are the best that life has to give.

Ellen Glasgow

I am thankful for laughter, except when milk comes out of my nose.

Woody Allen

laughter

*At the height of laughter, the universe is flung
into a kaleidoscope of new possibilities.*

Jean Houston

One of the best things in the world to be is a boy;
it requires no experience, but needs some practice to be a good one.

Charles Dudley Warner

l i v e l i n e s s

Boys are beyond the range of anybody's sure understanding, at least
when they are between the ages of 18 months and 90 years.

James Thurber

Boy, n.: a noise with dirt on it.

Not Your Average Dictionary

loudness

A child enters your home and for the next twenty years makes
so much noise you can hardly stand it. The child departs, leaving
the house so silent you think you are going mad.

John Andrew Holmes

Always kiss your children goodnight—even if they're already asleep.

H. Jackson Brown, Jr.

love

Children need love, especially when they do not deserve it.

Harold Hulbert

There comes a time in every rightly-constructed boy's life when he has
a raging desire to go somewhere and dig for hidden treasure.

Mark Twain

mischief

Children are a great comfort in your old age—
and they help you reach it faster, too.

Lionel Kauffman

Don't worry that children never listen to you;
worry that they are always watching you.

Robert Fulghum

perception

What a distressing contrast there is between the radiant intelligence
of the child and the feeble mentality of the average adult.

Sigmund Freud

You are worried about seeing him spend his early years in doing nothing. What!
Is it nothing to be happy? Nothing to skip, play, and run around all day long?
Never in his life will he be so busy again.

Jean-Jacques Rousseau

p l a y f u l n e s s

When I grow up I want to be a little boy.

Joseph Heller

*There is always one moment in childhood
when the door opens and lets the future in.*

Graham Greene

promise

Every child begins the world again.

Henry David Thoreau

Every genuine boy is a rebel and an anarch. If he were allowed to develop according to his own instincts, his own inclinations, society would undergo such a radical transformation as to make the adult revolutionary cower and cringe.

John Andrew Holmes

rebelliousness

Boyhood is a most complex and incomprehensible thing. Even when one has been through it, one does not understand what it was. A man can never quite understand a boy, even when he has been the boy.

Gilbert K. Chesterton

If you look in the eyes of the young, you see flame.

Victor Hugo

restlessness

Little children, headache; big children, heartache.

Italian proverb

The infinitely little have a pride infinitely great.

Voltaire

r i v a l r y

Taste the relish to be found in competition—
in having put forth the best effort within you.

Henry J. Kaiser

It kills you to see them grow up.
But I guess it would kill you quicker if they didn't.

Barbara Kingsolver

self-reliance

We've had bad luck with our kids—they've all grown up.

Christopher Morley

We think boys are rude, unsensitive animals but it is not so in all cases.
Each boy has one or two sensitive spots, and if you can find out where they are
located you have only to touch them and you can scorch him as with fire.

Mark Twain

s e n s i t i v i t y

You don't have to suffer to be a poet. Adolescence is enough suffering for anyone.

John Ciardi

A characteristic of the normal child is he doesn't act that way very often.

Author unknown

s i l l i n e s s

It's lovely to be silly at the right moment.

Horace

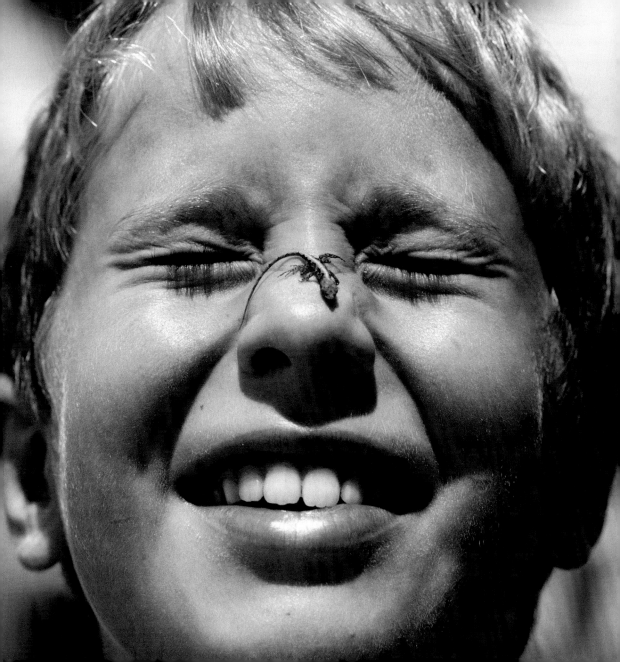

Mother Nature is providential. She gives us twelve years to develop
a love for our children before turning them into teenagers.

William Galvin

s l o p p i n e s s

The invention of the teenager was a mistake. Once you identify a period
of life in which people get to stay out late but don't have to pay taxes—
naturally, no one wants to live any other way.

Judith Martin

Children in a family are like flowers in a bouquet:
there's always one determined to face in an opposite
direction from the way the arranger desires.

Author unknown

stubbornness

You have to hang in there, because two or three years later, the
gremlins will return your child, and he will be wonderful again.

Jill Eikenberry

The finest qualities of our nature, like bloom on fruits, can
be preserved only by the most delicate handling.

Henry David Thoreau

t e n d e r n e s s

Children remind us to treasure the smallest gifts,
even in the most difficult of times.

Allen Klein

Allow children to be happy in their own way,
for what better way will they find?

Samuel Johnson

uniqueness

Little boys are like snowflakes, there are no two alike.

Author unknown

A boy is a magical creature—you can lock him out of your workshop,
but you can't lock him out of your heart.

Allan Beck

u n c o n d i t i o n a l
l o v e

In raising my children, I have lost my mind but found my soul.

Lisa T. Shepherd

5996